I THINK MY CAT IS BROKEN

A CAT LOVER'S COLLECTION OF SATIRICAL WISDOM ON CAT BEHAVIOR.

VIOLET EMBERSTONE

CONTENTS

Greetings   1

1. Gifts of Gruesome Gratitude   3
    Understanding Your Cat's Deliveries

2. The Loo Lookout   9
    Your Cat's Bathroom Surveillance Mission

3. Fluffed Up and Frazzled   14
    Decoding Your Cat's Bushy Tail Tales

4. To Coo or Not to Coo   20
    The Peculiar Pigeon-Like Purr of Your Cat

5. Claws and Effect   25
    Navigating Your Cat's Inner Freddy Krueger

6. The Feline Physics Professor   31
    Why Your Cat Loves Gravity

7. Moonlight Mischief   36
    The Nocturnal Antics of Your Feline Roommate

8. Tail-Shake Tango   42
    Unraveling Your Cat's Quirky Pre-Pounce Shimmy

9. Stealth Mode Activated   48
    Understanding Your Cat's Low-to-the-Ground Lurking

10. Hide and Seek   53
    The Secret World Inside Your Cat's Favorite Hiding Spots

11. Whispering Whiskers   58
    The Mysterious Symphony of Cat Purring

12. Kneading Love   63
    The Doughy Delights of Feline Affection

13. Cat Zoomies   69
    Fur-Fueled Frenzy

The End   74

About the author   76

References   77

GREETINGS

Welcome to a world where normalcy is as elusive as a cat in a game of hide-and-seek. If you've ever found yourself questioning the operational status of your feline friend, you're not alone. The notion of a 'broken' cat is the crux of our whimsical journey, a delightful exploration into the enigmatic behavior of our purring companions.

Think of a quiet evening, disrupted by your cat's sudden sprint across the room, chasing phantoms or perhaps just their own tail. Or those moments where your feline stares intently into the void, seemingly captivated by the secrets of the cosmos hidden in your living room. These peculiar antics might prompt you to wonder—is your cat just quirky or did it come with a few wires crossed?

Before you start looking for a customer service number for cats or a troubleshooting guide, let's muse over a few humorous considerations:

Have you ever lightly blown on your cat, hoping it might reboot like an old video game cartridge?

Have you searched their fluffy underbelly for a hidden 'reset' button, only to be greeted by a confused purr or a playful swat?

Have you fantasized about finding a user manual, perhaps conveniently hidden under their litter box?

Cats, in their majestic oddity, are more akin to a riddle wrapped in a mystery. Their bewildering behavior can make even the quirkiest of your acquaintances seem dull. From midnight zoomies to an inexplicable obsession with cardboard boxes, these four-legged enigmas challenge our understanding of 'normal' pet behavior.

But fear not, dear reader, for your cat is likely not broken. These eccentricities are the hallmarks of feline charm. Cats embody a unique blend of independence and affection, with a dash of capriciousness for good measure. Their peculiarities are not flaws, but rather expressions of their distinct personalities.

As you navigate this book, consider it an adventurous expedition into the heart of catdom. Imagine holding a question about your cat in your mind, then flipping open to a random page, guided by feline intuition.

Prepare to embark on a journey filled with laughter, bewilderment, and a newfound appreciation for the mysterious creatures that cats are. By the end, you might still not have all the answers (do we ever, when it comes to cats?). Still, you'll certainly view your enigmatic friend with a mix of admiration, amusement, and a deeper understanding of their quirky behavior.

So, let's dive into the fascinating world of 'Is my cat broken, or is it just being a cat?' The answer might surprise you, delight you, and most definitely entertain you. Welcome to the whimsical, wondrous, and occasionally weird world of cats.

CHAPTER ONE

GIFTS OF GRUESOME GRATITUDE

UNDERSTANDING YOUR CAT'S DELIVERIES

You step outside on a seemingly ordinary morning. The air is crisp, the sky a watercolor of dawn hues, but the serenity is abruptly shattered. There, on your doorstep, lies a chilling spectacle—a small, inert body. Your heart skips a beat. A toy? A sick joke? The unsettling reality slowly creeps in—this is no prank.

Your gaze fixates on the lifeless form. A bird, its wings forever stilled; a mouse, its scurrying days abruptly ended. A thousand questions whirl in your mind. How? Why? The scene before you feels like a macabre puzzle, each piece more disturbing than the last. Your morning coffee turns bitter in your mouth, the normalcy of your day tainted by this grim tableau.

Suspicion turns to your feline companion. That innocent, purring creature is now a prime suspect in this backyard crime scene. But why? What drives your seemingly cuddly pet to transform your doorstep into a scene straight out of a horror story? You ponder wild theories. Is your home built on an ancient feline burial ground? Has your cat joined a secret midnight hunters' guild?

Morbid Tokens of Affection

In your mind, you can almost hear your cat's voice, chillingly nonchalant "Look, Mommy, I brought you a nice bird. It was flying, but now it's not." The thought sends a shiver down your spine. Your once cozy home now feels like the setting of a nature horror show, where you're both the audience and the unwitting participant.

Amidst the shock and horror, a bizarre thought strikes you. In some twisted way, could this be your cat's version of a Valentine's Day gift? One that replaces roses with something that recently experienced the cycle of life. The idea is as unsettling as it is oddly endearing.

For those considering welcoming a cat into their lives, be prepared. It's not just about soft cuddles and gentle purrs. You're signing up for a role in a backyard drama, where you may find yourself burying small, feathered or furry actors in a makeshift cemetery. It's a role that requires a sturdy shovel and a strong stomach.

Why cats bring gifts

Crawlers

Might be mimicking your mother's nagging about the mess in your house. "Are you going for the rainforest vibe or the swamps? Snakes would pay to live here."

Winged

Could be your cat's way of saying, "I am your knight in shining armor. I'd slay dragons for you, but this bird will do for now."

Understanding Your Cat's Inner Vader

This isn't just a random act of feline mischief. There's something deeper and darker at play, a primal force manifesting in the most macabre of ways. Your cat, in its peculiar manner, is tapping into a wild, ancestral heritage. Perhaps you watch too many movies, or maybe, just maybe, you have a Sith Lord in the making.

But before we jump into the dark side, here are some tips to harness the force to keep your cat from turning.

Jedi Training

Keep your padawan busy with interactive play to steer their mind from murderous intentions.

Missions

Engage them with toys that move like prey, offering treats upon cap-
ture to mimic the sense of achievement and satisfaction of the hunt.

Meditation

Encourage indoor activities and create a sanctuary that even Yoda
would approve of, keeping them away from the temptation of the dark
side.

Being a custodian of a cat is a great responsibility—one that requires embracing both the light and dark sides of your furry bundle
and dealing with their natural tendency toward peculiarity and chaos.
It requires embracing the bizarre and the unexplainable, looking beyond the gruesome, appreciating the wild beauty in their acts, and
finding the bond and untold affection.

So, the next time you're faced with an unearthly offering at dawn,
remember, you're not just a pet owner. You're the chosen confidant
of a creature as mysterious as it is loving. A creature that, in its unique
way, trusts you enough to share the spoils of its hunt, even if those
spoils are more suited to a grave than a living room. And as you reach
for the shovel, perhaps with a mix of resignation and affection, you
realize that this is just another chapter in the wonderfully weird book
of living with a cat.

Welcome to the galaxy of cat keeping, where every day is an adventure and every gift a window into your cat's wild nature and guiltless pleasures—a darkness amidst soft purrs that even Vader would approve of.

Chapter Two

THE LOO LOOKOUT

Your Cat's Bathroom Surveillance Mission

You amble towards the bathroom, your fortress of solitude, only to be confronted by a silent sentinel. Those eyes, unblinking and calculating, belong to none other than your feline housemate, now moonlighting as a bathroom spy. This isn't a scene from a Hitchcock film; it's just Tuesday with your cat, the self-appointed guardian of the loo.

The bathroom has now become a feline surveillance hub. There, veiled by the shower curtain's shadow, sits your cat, an enigmatic figure. Those unwavering eyes seem to document your every move, conducting a scientific study titled Human Habits in the Loo: A Feline's

Perspective, or perhaps ensuring that you haven't been flushed away into oblivion.

 Your purring, affectionate creature showcases a level of patience that would impress even the most experienced stakeout agent. But what's the endgame? A bizarre attempt at companionship, maybe?

Nothing says solidarity like a friend sticking around during your loo break. Or perhaps it's an expression of their innate curiosity, a need to supervise and ensure everything is under control. You're safe and sound, not inadvertently caught in the whirlpool of the toilet or exploring the deeper end of your tub. The notion is both amusing and slightly disconcerting.

Lookout Stations: The Strategic Positions of a Bathroom Watcher

Behind the Curtain

Your cat's attempt at camouflage is like a National Geographic reporter on a mission. They're not just behind the curtain; they're deep undercover, observing humans in their natural habitat with the precision of a sharp investigator.

On the Floor in Front of You

This is an up-close and personal scientific study, not just of what you're doing but of your response to the added stimuli of an audience. It's a groundbreaking research project in their eyes, analyzing your every move with the intensity of a seasoned academic.

Perched on Higher Ground

Whether it's the sink or atop the bathroom dresser, this vantage point is a clear power move. It's a reminder that in the grand scheme of things, you're here by their grace. Every glance from on high says,

"Remember, human, I am the watcher, the guardian of realms, the keeper of the loo. Proceed with my blessing."

Mastering the Art of Privacy: A Guide to Feline Diplomacy

Set Boundaries (If You Dare)

It's a delicate dance of wills, where your attempts to establish bathroom privacy are met with the feline equivalent of a polite nod and a promptly ignored memo. Consistency might eventually pay off, or so you hope.

Distract and Divert (The Art of Misdirection)

The key to a moment's privacy may lie in a well-timed distraction. A strategically placed toy or an engaging activity outside the bathroom could buy you precious minutes of solitude. It's a sleight of hand that even Houdini would appreciate.

Create a Comfortable Space (The Peace Treaty)

Offering an alternative lookout post could be the olive branch that maintains peace. A cozy nook with a view, replete with all the comforts a cat could ask for, might just tempt them away from their bathroom post. It's a negotiation of comfort, a compromise that respects their surveillance needs while reclaiming your privacy.

Understanding the Triggers (Applying the Art of War)

In deciphering the enigma of your cat's bathroom fixation, consider the triggers. Is it the allure of running water, the solitude of the space, or simply the joy of your undivided attention? Understanding these motivations allows you to strategize, plan, and outmaneuver. In the grand chessboard of cat-human cohabitation, every move is a step toward mutual understanding.

As you navigate the daily adventures of living with a cat, embrace the quirks, the unexpected moments of companionship, and yes, even the bathroom espionage. It's a testament to the unique bond between cats and humans, a reminder that life with these enigmatic creatures is never dull.

So, the next time you find yourself under the watchful eye of your feline friend, remember that this is just one of the many joys of cat ownership, a story you'll one day recount with a smile and a shake of the head.

Chapter Three

FLUFFED UP AND FRAZZLED

Decoding Your Cat's Bushy Tail Tales

Y ou're unwinding in your living room, grateful to be alone with your thoughts, and looking forward to long hours of peace and quiet. The gentle purr of your feline companion provides the perfect background acoustics to the serene day you feel you deserve. But peace is a fleeting luxury. Suddenly, your cat undergoes a transformation reminiscent of a scene in Frankenstein—"it's alive!" Their tail, typically a sleek accessory, now blossoms into an extravagant, bushy spectacle. Is it a ghostly presence? Fear not!

To those new to the cat-keeping circle, or contemplating joining this exclusive society, witnessing a cat with its tail puffed to the size of a bottle brush might be puzzling or mildly alarming. It's quite normal to find yourself constructing absurd theories. For all you know, this fluffy display may be a new trending fashion statement, after all, in the human world, bushy eyebrows are making a comeback.

Truth be told that grandiose tail isn't merely a whimsical style choice by your feline. A cat's tail is a gauge of their internal climate, waving in the breeze of your cat's emotional tempests like a ghostly pennant in a haunted castle. Fear is the most common bush tail inducer, transforming your serene Mr. Fluffy into Sir Fluff-Tail of Camelot, ready to defend his realm from unforeseen invaders—or perhaps hide under the sofa, plotting their next stealthy move.

But navigating your cat's squirrel tail is like unraveling a puzzle in a fur coat. In the wild, cats use their tails as communicative tools. Within your home, this behavior morphs into a multifaceted dialect, as complex and varied as the spells in a witch's grimoire, articulating a spectrum of emotions from sheer elation to caution.

Deciphering the Bushy Tail: Appreciating Your Cat's Bad Hair Day

Your cat's tail is akin to a furry oracle, forecasting the emotional weather with more enigma than a cryptic crossword puzzle. Let's decode these mystical signs and dive into the feline psyche.

The Bottle Brush

Often a sign of fear or defensive aggression. Imagine your cat has just encountered the ghost of catnip past. Either that, or they're rehearsing for a role in Phantom of the Opera: Feline Edition.

The Playful Plume

Suggests excitement and joy. It's as if your cat is hosting a midnight soirée for spectral guests, twirling their tail like a dapper ghost about to break into a moonlit waltz.

The Curious Quiver

Signals cautious interest. Your cat might be pondering the mysteries of the universe or contemplating the perplexing nature of your new decor.

The Agitated Tuft

Indicates a threat and readiness to defend. It's best to give them space unless you're prepared for a close encounter of the furry kind. Remember, it's all fun and games until the claws come out!

Taming the Tail: Tips for the Haunted Human

Managing your cat's bushy tail behavior is akin to being the director of a paranormal play. Here's how to embrace their fluffy escapades while maintaining household harmony.

Observe and Learn

Like deciphering a Da Vinci cipher, identifying the precursors to your cat's bushy tail can help you anticipate and manage their reactions. It's like reading tea leaves, except furrier and with more attitude.

Create a Calm Environment

Aim for a cozy cat castle vibe, transforming your home into a stress-free sanctuary where even the most skittish feline spirit can unwind.

Engage in Play

Regular playtime can help your cat exorcise their pent-up energy. It's like a séance, but instead of summoning spirits, you're conjuring up joy and preventing your living room from turning into a nocturnal battleground.

Provide Safe Spaces

Offer cozy hideaways for your cat to retreat and ponder the enigmas of their nine lives, or perhaps just plot their next grand escapade. It's their personal bat cave—a sanctuary from the mundane.

Consider the tale of Mr. Coco, a tabby who amuses with his dramatic tail expressions. His human, intrigued by his antics, began chronicling the various 'tail moods' of Mr. Coco, crafting a humorous yet enlightening guide for fellow cat enthusiasts. From the Monarch of the Living Room fluff during playtime to the Cucumber Conundrum fright-fluff, Mr. Coco's tail narrates its own captivating saga.

Then there's Luna, a Siamese renowned for her theatricality. Luna's human narrates stories of her tail morphing into a regal plume whenever she's on the prowl for that elusive laser dot. In Luna's realm, the chase for the red dot is an epic adventure, vividly narrated through her body language. It's as if each pounce and leap is part of her audition for Dancing with the Stars: Feline Edition.

Embrace the hairy drama that each tail show infuses into your life. In the grand narrative of cat companionship, the tales told by the tail are mere chapters in an endless saga that will keep you turning pages.

So, the next time your cat's tail transforms into a bushy spectacle, appreciate the complexity and depth of this behavior. It's not just a bad hair day; it's a captivating dance of communication that gives you insights into your cat's world. Either that or it's a foreboding sign of an unexpected visitor.

CHAPTER FOUR

TO COO OR NOT TO COO

THE PECULIAR PIGEON-LIKE PURR OF YOUR CAT

Whisker twitches, soothing purrs, and the occasional *cat-aclysmic* knock of objects falling victim to playful paws and the laws of gravity—these are the ambient sounds of a household graced by a cat. However, for some cat owners, an additional, more intriguing sound complements this symphony: the coo of a cat. Yes, a coo, a sound that might prompt a curious glance around for feathers or a quick check for hidden portals to a pigeon-ruled realm. It is with distinct pleasure that this chapter introduces you to cats who moonlight as pigeon impersonators.

Previously on "Pigeons: The Untold Feline Fantasy," an unassuming cat servant enjoys his day in the backyard. Perched on his favorite hammock, a freshly squeezed lemonade in hand, and his phone switched to silent mode, he is unexpectedly serenaded by a questioning coo. Coo who? "Did I accidentally bring a pigeon home?" he asks no one in particular. He looks at the cat. The cat looks back, its lips forming around a distinct yet undeniable coo.

For those who have encountered the feline coo, you may be tempted to question your reality. "Have I stumbled into an alternate universe where cats are the new pigeons?" or "Is this a glitch in the matrix?" Contrary to what you think, your cat remains the same standard edition, without sprouting wings or pecking at the dirt. Apparently, the coo is not trademarked by the Pigeon Constitutional Council, and your cat cooing does not defy any laws of nature.

Comprehending the Coos: A Feline Linguist's Guide

Diving into cat coos is like cracking the code of a secret society where every "coo" is a cryptic message or a hidden handshake. Let's decode this feline Morse code with a guide that's part mystery, part comedy skit.

The Morning Melody Coo

A cryptic summons that translates to, "Arise, humble servant! The sun has audaciously climbed the sky without seeking my paw of approval."

The Contented Chirp-Coo

A mysterious concoction of purr and plot, it's your cat's way of saying, "The realm is peaceful, but beware, for I'm planning my next adorable onslaught."

The Attention-Seeking Coo

This insistent coo is your cat's royal decree: "Halt, mere mortal! Your undivided attention is required at my whiskered court, posthaste!"

The Puzzled Pigeon Coo

A thoughtful coo that leaves you wondering whether your cat is unraveling the fabric of the cosmos or merely critiquing your wardrobe.

The Explorer's Echo Coo

Echoing from the depths of uncharted realms (like the mysterious underbelly of your sofa), this coo is your brave explorer's message: "Fear not, for though I tread in shadow, my whiskers shall light the way back home."

When you've got a cooer, you've got a cat who defies the ordinary. Not even the Sorcerer Supreme could conjure a reality where these enchanting sounds don't resonate through your living space. Cooing is not just a habit; it's a personality trait, well shaken and stirred into the essence of your cat's being.

Consider yourself among the fortunate few, for you're in the presence of a multilingual whiskered companion. As they twirl their whiskers in their furry paws, they might as well be asking, "How many languages do you speak?" Their coos, chirps, and trills are the melodic verses of a language that transcends human understanding, a secret dialogue between the realms of the known and the mystical.

Consider Jasper, a Maine Coon whose dawn coos harmonize with the birds outside, painting auditory masterpieces that blur the lines between nature and feline fantasy. His human, both amused and intrigued, has come to view these performances as Jasper's way of connecting with the world beyond the window, a symphony composed in the key of mystery.

Then there's Bella, a Siamese mix known for her midnight melodies. Her coos, under the silver glow of the moon, weave a tapestry of sound that's both comforting and cryptic, a serenade that speaks of affection entwined with an acknowledgment of something other-worldly.

Each coo and purr isn't just background noise; it's a soundtrack in the ongoing dramedy of living with cats—a narrative that spins from enchanting to "Did my cat just try to summon a pigeon spirit?"

Next time your living room echoes with a cat coo, take a beat to enjoy the absurdity. It's not merely a cat randomly making sounds; it's your personal whiskered artist inviting you to a private concerto. No need for detective gear or ancient texts to decipher this; just lean into the delightful melody of your talented and expressive cat.

CHAPTER FIVE

CLAWS AND EFFECT

NAVIGATING YOUR CAT'S INNER FREDDY KRUEGER

Ah, the world of cat ownership, where your plush couch doubles as a sacrificial altar for feline claw rituals. Here, we delve into the enigmatic art of cat scratching, a blend of innate instinct, territorial marking, and a dash of creativity.

Envision your living space under the bewitching moonlight, a sanctuary of serenity now vulnerable to nocturnal whims. Lurking in the shadows is your cat, eyes glinting with mischief and primal urge. The couch, once a pristine symbol of comfort, now stands as the chosen canvas for their new masterpiece.

As your cat sidles up to the couch, they whip out their claws—those fur-clad weapons. The couch, innocent and unsuspecting, lets out a silent, fabric-ripping scream with every slash. It's like watching a fluffy shredder at work in your living room, where each meticulously plotted scratch is a masterclass in couch destruction.

For your tiny Freddy Krueger in fur, the enthusiastic evisceration of your sofa or those designer cushions isn't a flare-up of kitty angst. No, it's their purr-fectly feline way of saying, "I hereby claim you and this cushy domain as mine, though a touch of redecoration by claw might be in order." It's less about feline fury and more an acknowledgment, "Yes, I deem you worthy of my majestic presence, but let's add some custom claw art to the decor, shall we?"

The Slasher Story Chronicles: Unraveling the Clawing Ritual

In the unsettling calm of dawn, your cat, a symbol of innocence, uncovers the horrors of the night. As you stumble upon the crime scene, a silent scream worthy of the best horror flicks escapes you. Your once-pristine sofa now bears the scars of a midnight massacre, its cotton entrails spilled out in a silent plea for mercy.

You look at your cat as it rolls gleefully on the floor, seemingly elated by the pain of your sofa and the shock on your face. You wonder what goes on in your cat's mind as it drags its claws through your innocent furniture. Let's dive in.

Marking Territory

Scratching is a way of keeping their claws trimmed and sharp, but it's not just about that, it's also a feline's way of claiming their space, a declaration of, "This couch is under new management."

Sensory Ecstasy

For your cat, every stroke is a sensory exploration, a journey through a world of textures. If you're a keen observer, you'd realize your cat has preferences when it comes to its victims. Whether it's your canvas bean bag or your ultra-soft 100% high-quality Egyptian cotton comforter, your cat's choice boils down to some personal criteria that can only be uncovered after careful forensic analysis of the shreds of evidence.

Art and Expression

Your cat isn't destroying; they're creating. In their mind, your couch is a canvas, and they're the Picasso of the cat world. Scratching is an individual ritual and may as well be an individual expression, and your little artist can be picky in choosing someone to collaborate with on a masterpiece. This is why in multi-cat homes, it's not often that cats can share a community scratching post.

Witness Protection Program: Slasher-Proofing Your Night

To survive this nocturnal ritual, let's conjure up some practical magic:

Enchanted Scratching Posts

Place scratching posts strategically sprinkled with catnip—the feline equivalent of the eye of a newt and the toe of a frog—to make them irresistible.

Protective Runes

Employ cat deterrents to shield your furniture from their magical claws. Sticky tapes, foil, or sprays can work like protection spells on your treasured decor.

Trim the Talons

Regularly trim their claws, akin to taming the talons of a mini dragon, to prolong your furnishings' life expectancy. Keeping their nails in check will keep them from booking a mani-pedi with your reading chair.

Stepping into the world of cat ownership? Buckle up; It's like having the Fab 5 take over your interior design, aiming for *tabby chic*. 'I think the feathers are better in the air than in your pillow. The cushion entrails on the floor open up the space, don't you think? Expect middle-of-the-night alerts akin to a dramatic scene from a home improvement show gone rogue: your Persian rug dramatically declaring, "I've been savagely redesigned! Immediate restoration is needed. Find me sprawled across the living room, next to the coffee table, gasping for aesthetics."

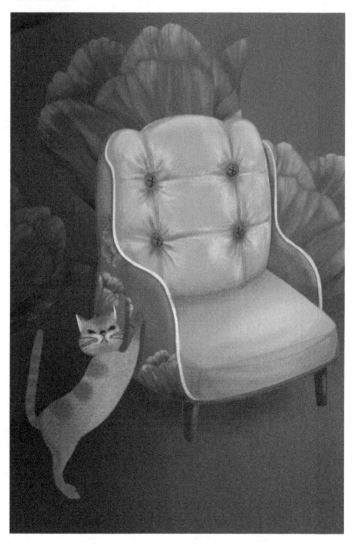

For the cat parenting veterans, each claw mark on the sofa is less of a vandalism act and more of a creative input from your feline housemate. If you catch them in the act of midnight redecorating and still manage to laugh, even as you mentally tally up the repair costs, congratulations! You've just unlocked the pro-level in the cat-keeping circle.

Life with a cat is an emotional adventure filled with unexpected twists and loops, punctuated by moments of panic when you discover their latest *masterpiece*. Remember, if you didn't cat-proof it, it's fair game for their claws. Just be sure to set your coffee down during breakfast, lest your cat's new artwork takes your breath away—quite literally.

Chapter Six

THE FELINE PHYSICS PROFESSOR

Why Your Cat Loves Gravity

Ah, the sound of porcelain crashing on your polished granite floor, a symphony conducted by none other than your cat, the furry Einstein. This daily spectacle of ludicrous genius meets sheer calamity—a gravity game that never fails to amuse and astound.

Picture this: your cat, the whiskered physicist, scrutinizes their realm with a calculating gaze. The unsuspecting target? An innocent trinket teetering on the edge, blissfully unaware of its impending doom and destined to reincarnate as dust on your floor.

While we humans accept gravity as a fundamental force, your cat remains a delightful skeptic. Each day is a new chapter in their cosmic quest, a narrative where the "what ifs" are explored with relentless curiosity. "Test subject number one thousand five hundred and fifty-two charted a unique trajectory through the void. Intriguing. Most intriguing," notes your cat, the intrepid explorer of the unknown.

This inquisitive nature sparks fanciful questions. "Where do cats truly hail from?" you ponder. In a world where human technology has leaped forward, could it be that our feline friends harbor secrets of extraterrestrial origins? Are they, perhaps, the true architects of our advancements, masquerading in plain sight as our beloved pets?

The Truth is Out There: Unraveling the Enigma Behind the Great Fall

The Hunt's Call

This isn't mere mischief; it's a primal rehearsal, a nod to their wild ancestry where every swipe and pounce meant survival.

Curiosity

That killed the... well, thankfully not the cat, but certainly the vase. Each tumble is a small step for your cat, one giant leap for feline-kind.

Entertainment

In your cat's world, physics is not just about gravity; it's about levity and amusement. "Will this vase defy the laws of gravity today?" wonders your cat, the mischievous scientist.

Attention

Amidst the humdrum of daily life, the sudden crash is a dramatic reminder from your cat: "Your sovereign requires admiration. Now."

If the cacophony of falling decor isn't quite your melody, fear not. There are ways to harmonize your living space with your cat's inquisitive nature.

Crafting Harmony with a Feline Physicist

Secure the Valuables

Protect your treasures from becoming accidental casualties in your cat's gravity experiments.

Designated Havoc Havens

Offer safe zones where your cat can unleash their curiosity without wreaking havoc in your living space.

Engaging Alternatives

Entice your cat with toys that echo the unpredictable movements of prey, captivating their attention and sparing your household items.

In the quiet aftermath of your cat's latest discovery, an unspoken accord forms between you two. You acknowledge their insatiable need to explore and challenge the unknown, and in return, they grace you with moments of laughter, reflection... and the urge to launch the occasional airborne slipper.

For newcomers to the realm of cat ownership, prepare for a life sprinkled with delightful disarray—a whimsical journey akin to Alice's wonderland. For the seasoned cat guardian, each toppled item is not a casualty but a charming testament to your cat's vibrant and inquisitive spirit.

Sharing your space with a cat is like living with a curious, playful entity with a knack for cosmic mischief. Their antics, while occasionally turning your world upside down, are the heartbeat of cat ownership. Perhaps, in a past life, your cat was the ringleader of celestial pranksters or a mystical force balancing the scales of the universe, one toppled vase at a time.

So, when you're picking up the pieces after your cat's latest encounter with gravity, remember: you're not just cleaning up, you're part of a study that aims to alter the fabric of reality as we know it; an endeavor that transforms every day into a topsy-turvy delight.

Chapter Seven

MOONLIGHT MISCHIEF

The Nocturnal Antics of Your Feline Roommate

In the quiet of the night, when shadows start to gossip with the glow of the streetlights, a special shadow moves with purpose. This isn't Batman; it's someone far less brooding, infinitely sneakier, and undeniably furrier. As the outside world dozes off, inside, a different kind of energy awakes. At the stroke of midnight, your cat, pretending to be a fluffy version of Nightwing, takes over. Suddenly, your quiet home turns into its own Gotham City, ready for a night full of sneaky adventures, mysterious escapades, and a whole lot of mischief.

Envision your living space, tranquil by day, now morphing into a shadowy playground under the moon's vigilant gaze. Here, your cat takes center stage, the house bathed in moonlight becoming a backdrop for their feline ballet. The performance begins with the pitter-patter of paws—a prelude to a symphony of sounds: the orchestrated thud of a vase, "Hello, my pretty. I'll make sure you fall... and your dog too," the rustle of curtains swaying to an unseen force, and perhaps the eerie echo of a solitary meow calling for your attention.

But these aren't mere antics of mischief and play; they stem from your cat's ancestral lineage. Each leap and bound, each curious investigation, carries a hint of the arcane. In these solitary hours, your cat seems to commune with the spirits of their wild ancestors, reenacting age-old rituals under the cover of darkness.

And yet, there's undeniable humor in these shadowy pursuits. Imagine your cat as a mysterious carnival fortune teller foreshadowing the demise of your custom wedding photo frame, or a spirit medium chasing delightful conversations with the unseen. Curiosity scuttles in the shadowy corners of your abode, but it won't kill the cat. The only victim here is the tranquility of your evening.

Tales From the Witching Hour: Anecdotes of Nocturnal Mischief

Professor Whiskerplot's Gravity Experiment

By day, a dignified feline scholar; by night, a relentless researcher of the Paws and Effect theory. Professor Whiskerplot conducts nightly gravity checks, ensuring that the laws of physics still apply to your favorite coffee mug. His methodology is simple yet effective: a swift paw swipe followed by a contemplative gaze at the shattered results.

Lady Fluffington's Midnight Ballet

As the clock strikes twelve, Lady Fluffington trades her daytime throne for the moonlit stage of your living room. Her performance is a mesmerizing mix of feline grace and sudden acrobatics, often culminating in the dramatic descent of your curtain—her favorite dance partner.

Sir Purr-a-lot's Eerie Serenades

While most cats prefer the silent hunt, Sir Purr-a-lot fancies himself a nocturnal vocalist. His repertoire ranges from haunting meows to mysterious trills, turning each night into an impromptu concert that leaves you wondering if you're hosting a ghostly choir or just a very vocal cat.

Unveiling the Mystique: Why Cats Embrace the Night

What drives these enigmatic creatures to turn our homes into their nocturnal playgrounds? Beyond the entertainment and ancestral instincts lies a complex tapestry of reasons.

The Call of the Wild

Domestication hasn't fully tamed the hunter within. Your living room, in the stillness of the night, resembles the vast savannas and forests that call to your cat's wild heart. Maybe you should schedule a more regular tidying up.

Sensory Exploration

Cats are creatures of the senses. The night amplifies their tactile, auditory, and visual experiences and makes every texture, sound, and movement an exciting discovery.

Bonding on Their Terms

Cats are known for their independent spirit, but they also seek connection. Those midnight meows and gentle headbutts might just be their way of saying, "You're part of my tribe."

Managing Your Furry Vigilante: A Guide to Peaceful Nights

For peaceful cohabitation with your night-time prowler, a tactical approach is essential for synchronizing your slumber schedules. Here's a nocturnal peace treaty plan.

Embrace the Sun

Amp up your cat's day with engaging activities and playtime to burn off that tireless energy. The goal? An exhausted cat by sundown.

Craft a Sleep Sanctuary

Infuse their evening retreat with calming scents like lavender or set up a snug nook that screams comfort. This isn't just a bed; it's a feline luxury spa.

Dinnertime Decoy

A hearty meal served as the stars come out plays into their natural cycle—eat, then sleep. Think of it as a culinary lullaby, leading them not into temptation but to dreamland.

Managing a creature of the night doesn't have to end with eye bags and a permanent 'just got out of bed' look on a daily basis. However, prepare for warm, unexpected cuddles on your head, sudden pounces that test the strength of your stomach, or a gentle paw tap on your face that says, "Wake up, the night is young!"

When the quiet of your room is pierced by the sound of mysterious movements or the faint echo of a meow, let a smile break through your drowsiness. As you lie there, wondering, "Is it a cat burglar or just... the cat? Should I grab a baseball bat or the catnip?"

Embrace your role as the Alfred to your cat's Batman—though you might question if Alfred ever managed to get a full night's sleep. Each nocturnal escapade, every shadowy pursuit, attests to the wild, imaginative spirit of your feline. Those middle-of-the-night wake-up calls, whether they're a soft paw on your cheek or an urgent meow, are your cat's way of including you in their world of mystery and adventure... or instructions to send the Batmobile.

Chapter Eight

TAIL-SHAKE TANGO

Unraveling Your Cat's Quirky Pre-Pounce Shimmy

A serene evening unwinds, soaked in the rebellion of a calo-
rie-count defiant dinner. You're sprawled out, the only intru-
sion on your tranquility being the foreboding thought of tomorrow's gym session. Then, in the midst of your serene contemplation,
the inexplicable occurs. Your cat, usually the epitome of feline grace,
suddenly seems inspired to showcase their own rendition of a dance.
It's as if they're saying, "Forget the gym, here's my workout." In one
fluid motion, they transition from regal poise to what appears to be a
rehearsal for the MTV Music Awards.

As your cat's hindquarters wiggle with an enthusiasm that would
surely draw nods from pop legends, a flurry of questions whirl

through your mind: "Is that tail shake directed at me, young lady?" Could this be a dance for a deluge of treats, or perhaps a warm-up for their grand debut on Feline TikTok? Is your living room on the verge of transforming into the backdrop for the internet's next sensation, or perhaps a cat-centric breakdance showdown?

The Tail-Shake Tango: Breaking Down the Dance Move

While your cat's pre-pounce shimmy might seem like a spontaneous burst of feline whimsy, it's actually a meticulously choreographed routine that would make the most seasoned dance instructors proud.

Ancestral Echoes

This dance is your cat's tribute to their wild ancestors, a compact, living room-friendly version of a jungle hunt. It's a rehearsal for the big catch, where the prey is a toy mouse or an unfortunate houseplant.

Sensory Checkpoint

Each tail twitch and body wriggle is your cat conducting a systems check "Thrusters ready? Check! Tail set to stun? Check!" It's like watching a pilot doing a pre-flight routine, except this flight navigates the treacherous terrain of your living room.

Whisker-Twitching Excitement

The anticipation of the hunt sends a thrill through their whiskers. This isn't just about catching the *prey*; it's about the drama of the chase, the crescendo of a perfectly executed pounce.

Cat Shimmy 101: Decoding the Dance

Diving into the feline ballet's intricacies, let's crack open a field guide to the choreography.

Step Right, Step Left

This alternating hindquarter dance step doesn't only lay the rhythmic foundation; it's their paw preparation for aerial maneuvers. A testament to their agility and readiness for the impending leap.

Tail Swing

As your cat's tail elegantly sweeps through the air, curling with grace at each pass, it's not merely a spectacle. This action serves a practical purpose, akin to a weathervane gauging the wind's direction but with far greater accuracy. It's a testament to their mastery over their environment, a delicate balance of grace and precision.

Tail Tap

This might initially strike you as a peculiar habit, a tail's erratic tap against the surface. Yet, it's far from a mere call for attention. This tapping is a blend of excitement and a unique form of communication. Like a Morse code, it sends vibrations through the ground, a message to unseen recipients, "I've found something thrilling, and it's mine."

The thrill of the hunt isn't just a metaphor—it literally sends vibrations of excitement from their whiskers down to their tail. And yet, this dance transcends mere physical prowess. As the human lucky enough to witness this spectacle, you're treated to a unique show that feels like a mash-up of So You Think You Can Dance and a late-night comedy improv. Every sway, every precise gyration seems to be your cat's way of boasting, "Bet you've never seen moves like these!" It's a moment where the anticipation of the chase transforms into a display of their inner pop star, ready for the spotlight.

But let's cut through the chuckles for a moment. This tail-shaking extravaganza is more than just a bid for internet fame; it's a deep dive into the duality of catdom. One minute, your furry friend is the epitome of grace, the next, they're doing the feline equivalent of breaking out the electric slide at a family reunion. It's this stark contrast between regal repose and dance floor dynamo that makes the tail-shake tango an endlessly entertaining enigma.

For those stepping into the furred fray of cat ownership, prepare for your home to be transformed into a dance studio where the dress code strictly includes fur. And for the seasoned cat aficionados, each tail twirl is a reminder that beneath the soft exterior lies a heart that beats to the rhythm of the wild—a soul that dances on the edge of domesticity and untamed mystique.

When the music starts and your cat hits the dance floor, embrace the show. This isn't just another cat quirk; it's a headline act in the carnival of life with a cat. Each performance is an invitation to laugh, to marvel, and to dance along in the shared rhythm of your unique domestic symphony. After all, what's life with a cat if not an ongoing dance-off, where every step, shuffle, and shimmy enriches your shared existence?

CHAPTER NINE

STEALTH MODE ACTIVATED

UNDERSTANDING YOUR CAT'S LOW-TO-THE-GROUND LURKING

As the evening shadows grow long and the twilight serenity of your home settles in, your once lazy, sunbathing furball morphs into a creature of stealth and mystery. Yes, your cat, adopting the finesse of a feline 007, becomes a whiskered 'James Bond,' prowling with the grace and precision of an undercover agent on a top-secret mission.

But this isn't your average spy story. Oh no. This is License to Purr. As your furry agent glides through the house, belly low and whiskers twitching, you can't help but wonder: is this a practice run for Mission

Impawsible? Are they on the trail of the elusive red dot, or perhaps plotting a covert operation to retrieve the heavily guarded treat jar?

Picture this: your house transforms into a scene straight out of a feline action movie. Your cat, the star of the show, demonstrates stealth tactics that would make Ethan Hunt proud. Each silent step, every calculated pause, would make anyone think your living room has become a high-stakes laser grid, visible exclusively through your cat's eyes equipped with elite spy optics.

Cracking the Code of Feline Stealth

Let go of the idea that your cat's sly actions stem from being trained as a member of the League of Shadows. This level of stealth isn't an added feature or a special order; it's standard issue, straight out of the box your feline agent came in. Your living room isn't just a living room; it's the backdrop for high-stakes espionage, where every shadow and corner holds the potential for intrigue and adventure.

Ancestral Instincts

Your cat's stealth mode isn't just for show. It's a deep-rooted tribute to their wild ancestors, where blending with the shadows was the key to survival. In the modern-day jungle of your home, these instincts translate into silent stalks and ghost-like appearances.

Sensory Mastery

Each calculated move, every silent step, is a testament to their sophisticated sensory network. Your cat sees the world as an endless adventure, where every sound, texture, and scent is a puzzle to solve.

The Element of Surprise

Life, for your cat, is an endless mission, with surprise as their ace in the hole. Be it a sudden leap onto an unsuspecting toy or a stealthy creep up on your lap, they're the masters of unpredictability, always ready to add a twist to the plot.

Yet, the true show isn't just in their ability to slip undetected behind enemy lines or execute a perfect surveillance operation. The real showstopper is the comedic brilliance that unfolds in the process. One second, your cat is the sleek, sophisticated spy, all poise and mystery. The next, they're the daredevil action hero, executing dramatic leaps and striking poses worthy of a movie poster (or an entry to America's funniest videos), declaring to the world, "Danger is not just my middle name—it's my calling card."

Navigating the World of Feline Espionage

As your home turns into the set of the latest feline action blockbuster, here are some tips to keep the peace and enjoy the show.

Designate Safe Zones

Create no-paw zones for your cat's nighttime escapades. A dedicated play area with plenty of toys and hideouts can turn into their personal MI6 headquarters.

Engage in Interactive Missions

Keep your cat's spy instincts satisfied with interactive toys and puzzles. It's like giving James Bond his next high-tech gadget—irresistible and bound to keep them occupied.

Decode the Signals

Decoding your cat's signals isn't just for laughs—it's a strategic move to protect your treasures. It's about understanding their wild whispers to distract them at the right moment. When you see your cat sizing up a potential victim (like your favorite mug), it's your cue to divert their attention. A quick toy toss can be the difference between safe decor and a cleanup mission.

Living with a cat is like living in a dojo, where your cat endlessly trains to master Ninja shadow techniques. If you have a cat who's a pro at stealth mode, prepare for silent stalks, surprise attacks, and missing trinkets.

When you spot your cat sneaking around, take a moment to enjoy their skills and take notes. Get ready to decode your cat's stealth signals, not just to marvel at their espionage excellence, but to perhaps save that precariously perched decor on the shelf or to save your foot from a playful surprise paw swipe from under the bed.

CHAPTER TEN

HIDE AND SEEK

THE SECRET WORLD INSIDE YOUR CAT'S FAVORITE HIDING SPOTS

Welcome to the whimsical world of your cat, the enigmatic Houdini of your household. Here, vanishing acts are routine, and every day is an episode of The Invisibility Chronicles.

As you're knee-deep in your latest TikTok dance challenge or deeply engrossed in a binge-watching marathon, a sudden silence descends. Your feline companion, once the star of your Instagram stories, has vanished into thin air.

Your chill home turns into something out of a weird detective show. Beneath the couch? A landscape reminiscent of a deserted planet, but devoid of feline life. Behind the curtains? A plot twist—no cat, just a few relics of your abandoned New Year's resolutions. Then, in a climactic reveal worthy of a Netflix special, you discover them. Nestled in an improbable fortress of solitude, your cat meets your gaze with a look that's part "What do you want?", part "Is it time for treats?"

The Cat Unwrapped: Inside the Mind of a Feline Houdini

You can't help but muse if your cat's vanishing prowess comes from an overindulgence in mysteries of magic or perhaps, clandestine attendance at wizardry workshops. Their nightly disappearances transcend mere quirky behavior, unfolding into a spectacle that could easily outshine the most skilled magician.

Unseen and Uncaptured

In the grand theater of the wild, being unseen was the key to survival. Today, that instinct manifests in your living room, transforming everyday nooks into secret sanctuaries.

Liquid Contortionists

Ever wondered if your cat is part liquid? Their ability to squeeze into the most improbable spaces confirms it. Whether it's an empty pizza box (a tribute to last night's binge) or the precarious gap behind the bookshelf, your cat proves that when it comes to hideouts, they're the reigning champions.

Solitude Seekers

Beyond their physical prowess, these hideouts serve a higher purpose. It's your cat's way of saying, "I need a meow-ment." Here, in their secret havens, they find tranquility, away from the hustle and bustle of household life. It's their personal retreat, a cat-sized sanctuary where the world's drama can't find them.

Strategies for Coexisting With a Feline Houdini

Mastering the art of cohabitation with your enigmatic housemate requires a blend of ingenuity and understanding—a way to honor their need for solitude without turning your home into a labyrinth of lost treasures.

Craft Personal Retreats

Transform your space into a sanctuary of secluded spots. Envision your home as a network of serene retreats—a collection of bespoke hideaways where your cat can savor their solitude, far from the hustle and bustle of your daily activities.

The Pre-Settlement Sweep

Before you claim your spot for relaxation, take a moment for a comprehensive check. This ritual not only spares you the surprise of a hidden companion but also respects your cat's preference for undisturbed hideaways, be it under a cozy throw or nestled in a fort of cushions.

Inspire Solitary Play

Encourage your cat's preference for quiet contemplation away from The Great Sock Hunt and towards more solitary entertainment. Offer toys that cater to their contemplative side, transforming their quest for solitude into a peaceful pursuit, keeping both your cat and your belongings in blissful harmony.

Your home isn't just a home; it's a magician's playground. Cardboard boxes become elaborate escape chambers, the space under the couch a vanishing cabinet, and that mysterious middle-of-the-night silence? It's just the suspenseful pause before the grand finale, where they reappear, as if by magic, on your chest at 3 a.m.

Whether you're a rookie getting your first taste of cat-induced bewilderment or a seasoned vet well-versed in the art of locating vanished furballs, every day with your cat is a masterclass in mystification.

So, buckle up for the ride, and keep your eyes peeled for the next act. Be ready to applaud their latest feat of escapology—be it freeing themselves from the closed bathroom or making their collar disappear without a trace. And when you finally catch a glimpse of your elusive illusionist lounging nonchalantly on the fridge, remember to laugh. Because, in the end, living with a cat is less about understanding their magic and more about marveling at their ability to turn the mundane into a spectacle of awe and hilarity. After all, who needs TV when you've got a cat pulling off high-stakes illusions that would make even the most seasoned magicians scratch their heads in wonder?

Chapter Eleven

Whispering Whiskers

The Mysterious Symphony of Cat Purring

I magine a lazy evening, Netflix's casting its glow in your living room as you indulge in a bowl of microwave popcorn. Suddenly, amidst the binge-watching bonanza, a familiar vibration interrupts. It's not a late-night text; it's your cat, purring contentedly on your lap. You lift your cat—no vibration. You put them back, and the gentle rumble returns. A living, purring enigma.

You might find yourself wondering, "Did my cat eat my phone, or is there a knee massager hidden in its fur?" But no, this isn't a case of swallowed electronics. This vibration is scientifically known as a purr, and it's a signature trait of your feline friend.

The Purr Paradox: Unraveling the Feline Frequency

So, what's the deal with purring? Is it a secret Morse code, a mystical chant, or just your cat's way of claiming the remote? The truth is as layered as the plot of your favorite fantasy series.

Ancient Whispers, Modern Mystery

Purring has its roots in the dawn of feline time, where communication and healing were pivotal. Beyond signaling bliss, it's your cat's way of expressing chill vibes. But as you sit there, basking in their rhythmic rumble, don't dismiss the possibility of something deeper, almost otherworldly, about this purring phenomenon.

Sonic Healing

Step into a realm where cats are not just adorable furballs but beings with an almost mystical ability to self-heal. Each purr isn't just a cuddle cue but a healing vibration, and a testament to their resilience and mysterious nature. While cat purrs are said to heal their injuries, the therapeutic vibes of purring extend to humans, too, believed to promote healing in bones and tissues. So, when your cat purrs away in your lap, they're not just offering comfort; they're providing a dose of feline first-aid.

Purr-lore and Superstition

Sometimes, as your cat purrs, it feels like you've been roped into an ancient, spectral ritual. Cats, once deified and dreaded in equal measure, used purring as a bridge to other dimensions, a sound steeped in enigmatic folklore. Could your cat's purring be a hotline to the feline divine?

When your cat sets their purring frequency to *enchant*, it might be more than a mere expression of contentment. Perhaps it's a silent declaration of trust, a shared secret, or even a feline way of branding you as part of their tribe—a silent, ancient pact between you and your furry mystic.

Decoding the Purrs: Understanding the Vibrations

Purrs and Paws

These are the purrs you can't hear but can feel as your cat kneads with their paws, signaling contentment or joy, "I am happy here. You are not permitted to move. However, you are encouraged to pet me until further notice."

Lawnmower Purr

Also known as the soliciting purr, this purr is your wake-up call, "Get up and feed me, but know that I also love you, so I'll step on your face if you rise too quickly."

Stiff Purr

Delivered with an eerie stillness, these purrs are not meant for human ears but serve as a note of aggression, warning, or submission towards other felines or beings. They can send chills down your spine, a primal reminder of your cat's wild side.

Not all purrs are spun from the same mystical fabric. Sometimes, a cat's purr might hint at discomfort or unease. Learning to discern the subtle shades of your cat's purring is like cracking a code, a skill that deepens the bond you share with your whiskered enigma.

In the grand narrative of life with a cat, the purr intertwines joy, mystery, and a touch of the unknown. It's a reminder that in the quiet moments with your cat, you're part of something timeless, wild, and mystical.

So, the next time your feline friend's purring breaks the silence, take a moment to appreciate this marvel—a small yet profound testament to the extraordinary world that cats bring into our lives. Whether it's a whispered message from ancient times, a healing touch, or a shared secret between you and your cat, each purr confirms that you're within their circle of trust.

CHAPTER TWELVE

KNEADING LOVE

THE DOUGHY DELIGHTS OF FELINE AFFECTION

I magine settling into your favorite chair, a book in one hand and a warm cup of tea in the other. Just as you reach peak coziness, your feline friend decides it's the perfect moment to start their shift at the imaginary bakery set up on your lap. Welcome to the world of cat kneading, a curious blend of affection, comfort, and, well, pastry-making.

The Fine Art of Becoming a Croissant

But before we dive deeper, let's consider the pros and cons of being turned into your cat's personal baking project.

Pros

Unconditional Love

Being chosen as the kneading spot is like receiving a Michelin star in the cat world.

Warmth and Comfort

There's something undeniably cozy about a purring cat working your lap.

Stress Relief

It's hard to worry about life's troubles when you're watching a feline baker at work.

Cons

Unexpected Acupuncture

Those claws can turn a peaceful session into a surprising poke-fest.

The Late-Night Shift

Cats often decide that the best time for kneading is when you're about to fall asleep.

Laundry Increase

Your lap-turned-bakery requires frequent cleaning due to flour (fur) buildup.

Let's knead into the essence of why our feline companions practice this pastry chef performance. Far from aspiring to turn us into tomorrow morning's bread basket, this behavior stems from their kittenhood. The gentle press of paws once stimulated milk flow from their mother. Now, they're ensuring we're still a comforting presence, albeit in a less... liquid form.

When this kneading is paired with purring, it's less about mystical lore and more akin to a chef's humming in the kitchen, where the combination of movement and sound works to complete a masterpiece of relaxation and affection. It's a moment of pure bonding, a tactile and auditory ritual that strengthens the connection between you and your cat.

But when does this pastry-making session usually occur? Typically, during those quiet moments of reflection or relaxation, your fur baby decides it's prime time to engage in their kneading meditation. It's their way of unwinding, reconnecting with their inner peace, and sharing it with you.

Not All Kneads are Created Equal

The Love Knead

Gentle, rhythmic, and often accompanied by purring. This is the feline equivalent of a hug.

The Attention Knead

More insistent, possibly accompanied by meowing. This knead says, "Look at me, feed me, love me!"

The Comfort-Seeking Knead

Done on soft surfaces (including you), seeking the ultimate cozy spot.

So, if you ever find yourself pondering about the slightly possessive nature of your cat's kneading, remember, it's their way of saying you're an irreplaceable part of their world. Embrace the humor and warmth of being chosen. And should you ever wake up feeling a bit more biscuit-like than usual, take it as a sign of the deepest affection, a magical transformation only the most loved croissants—er, humans—can experience.

Surviving the Night Shift: Tips for Prospective Croissants

Wear Thick Clothing

To minimize the acupuncture effect.

Keep a Blanket Handy

For those moments when your cat's kneading becomes too enthusiastic.

Enjoy the Moment

Despite the surprise dough-making sessions, these moments are precious.

Embracing life with a cat is to understand that you're part of an ongoing, dynamic narrative—one where you might occasionally play the dough to their baker. But it's in these moments, as you find yourself being gently kneaded and purr-serenaded into relaxation, that you realize the true essence of feline affection. It's a quirky, tender, and sometimes prickly reminder of the unique bond shared with our whiskered companions.

So, the next time your personal feline baker decides it's time to check if you've risen enough to be considered a proper croissant, remember to take it as a high compliment. You're not just the caretaker of a cat; you're the muse for their culinary expressions of love, a living testament to their creative and affectionate endeavors.

Chapter Thirteen

CAT ZOOMIES

Fur-Fueled Frenzy

In the bewitching hours of cat o'clock, there unfolds a spectacle so frenzied it could rival the most chaotic of cartoons. Welcome to the world of the zoomies, where your usually composed cat morphs into a whirlwind on a fur-fueled mission. It's a comedy, a mystery, and a dash of the supernatural, all rolled into one fuzzy package. Let's dive into the madness, shall we?

Just when the world seems to slow down, your cat decides to break the sound barrier. One minute, they're a picture of serenity; the next, they're fur-clad Flash Gordon, Superman, and Shazam in a band. The question isn't who's faster; it's whether your living room can handle the speed.

The Midnight Marathon: Understanding the Zoom

Why do our serene companions suddenly engage in these zooming sprees? The reasons are as multifaceted as a cat's personality.

Pent-Up Purr Energy

Stored energy needs an outlet, and what better way than impersonating a furry speedster?

The Litter Box Victory Lap

Completing a successful bathroom break deserves a celebratory sprint, naturally.

Primal Playtime

Tapping into their inner pint-sized predator, they're not just running; they're on the prowl in the great urban jungle.

The Living Room Racetrack

Your home isn't just a home; it's the premier racetrack for your cat's zooming pleasure. Here's how to ensure it's up to code.

Breakable Beware

Secure anything that can't survive a feline frenzy. Think of your cat as a miniature bull in a china shop.

Create a Zoom-Safe Zone

Designate an area where your cat can safely unleash their inner Usain Bolt, free from the risk of knocking over your treasured tea set.

Engage and Redirect

Use interactive toys to channel their zoomies into a controlled yet equally satisfying, play session.

Despite the occasional mild disruption to our regular program—like the mystery of the broken picture frames—there's an undeniable joy in witnessing these zooming sprees. They're a reminder of our cats' untamed essence, a living link to their wild ancestors, all while being undeniably adorable.

Embracing the Whirlwind

Living with a zoomie-prone cat means embracing the unexpected with open arms—and maybe a cushion or two for safety. It's about finding the charm in the chaos and the moment in madness. After all, not everyone has a personal superhero capable of breaking the speed record from the kitchen to the couch.

Expect the Unexpected

Just when you think it's time to wind down, prepare for the zoomies. It's not just a cat thing; it's a superhero thing.

Laugh and Learn

Each zooming spree is an opportunity to learn more about your cat's personality and energy levels.

Join the Chase

Sometimes, the best way to enjoy the zoomies is to become part of the action. Just watch out for the hairpin turns.

As your cat gears up for their next whirlwind tour through the hallways, consider this not just a spectator sport but an open invitation. Why not try to outspeed your furry speedster? It's a challenge that might have you both racing through the house, adding laughter and excitement to your daily routine. Just be cautious—while darting around corners and sprinting down hallways, make sure you don't bend the fabric of time itself. After all, we wouldn't want to accidentally create a feline-flavored time paradox.

For those new to the cat-keeping circle, being visited by the zoomies is like having a tornado blow your house to the Emerald City, but in this case, the tornado is inside your house. Be sure to secure the lamps and the curtains as this racetrack will defy the laws of physics. Watch your fluffy kitty rev its engine and speed through the hall, bouncing on vertical walls, and clearing obstacles with anti-gravity techniques. For pro cat owners, the zoomies is an unavoidable part of the day when we tie our hair back, sit back and read a novel while the cats use the chandeliers as their circuit.

In the delightful escapade of living with a cat, remember: the zoomies aren't just random bursts of energy; they're the highlight of the day. So, lace up your sneakers and get ready to join in if you dare.

THE END

A nd so, we close the book on our feline escapades, a journey that
has taken us through the delightful, sometimes bewildering,
world of cats. Let's part ways (for now) with a touch of humor, a dash
of wit, and a purr of contentment, encapsulated in a lighthearted verse
to honor our whiskered companions.

In every corner, nook, and cranny,
lurk tales of feline fancy and folly,
with paws as soft as whispered dreams,
and schemes as wild as moonlit streams.
Oh, the sagas of whiskered whispers,
of zoomies, purrs, and midnight twisters,
of stealthy prowls and sudden leaps,
in the quiet world where the catnip creeps.
Behold the baker, kneading with glee,
turning laps into lands of doughy sea,

master chef in a fur-lined coat,
crafting biscuits on a note of droll.
And then the zoomies—a madcap race,
a feline flash, a breakneck chase,
through halls and rooms, they romp and dash,
in a whirlwind ballet, a midnight bash.
In repose, they purr, a rumbling tune,
a melody beneath the crescent moon,
a whisper of ancient, mystical lore,
a healing hum, a feline roar.
Their eyes, aglow with a curious sheen,
reflecting worlds unseen,
in their gaze, a story untold,
of legends, myths, and heroes bold.
So, as we part from this tale of tails,
of furry antics and curious trails,
let's toast to the cats–our friends, our muses,
the authors of laughs, the keepers of ruses.
May this ode to our quirky feline kin,
leave you with a smile, a chuckle, a grin.
for in the dance of whiskers and paws,
we find life's joy, its simplest cause.
As you turn this final, whimsical page,
may the memory of these tales gently age,
and in the laughter and love they endow,
may you always hear the cat's soft meow.

·♥·♥·♥·♥·♥·

ABOUT THE AUTHOR

 Born with an innate affection for all creatures great and small, our author grew up amidst an eclectic assortment of pets – furred, finned, scaled, and shelled companions. Her fascination with felines was love at first sight; over the years in her ancestral home, she has welcomed over 13 cats into her heart. Now residing with her family in the verdant kingdom of Cambodia, she shares her home with two rescue cats: Oreo and Momo. She fills her days painting, writing, playing chase-the-yarn games with her cats, and chuckling at her own jokes. Her experience caring and living with cats combined with a distinctive sense of humor are brilliantly reflected in "I Think My Cat Is Broken." This book offers not only valuable insights but also entertaining anecdotes that will delight both new cat owners and seasoned feline enthusiasts alike.

REFERENCES

Bartels, M. (2023, October 7). *Why do cats knead like they're making biscuits?* Scientific American. https://www.scientificamerican.com/article/why-do-cats-knead-like-theyre-making-biscuits/

Cat zoomies: The bizarre behavior explained. (2023). Four Paws. https://www.fourpaws.com/pets-101/cat-corner/cat-zoomies-explained

Comstock, J. (2023, August 23). *What are the cat zoomies and why do cats get them?* Daily Paws. https://www.dailypaws.com/cats-kittens/behavior/common-cat-behaviors/cat-zoomies

Garcia, M. F. (2022, October 17). *Cat has a habit of twerking but experts say there's a reason why.* Animal Channel. https://animalchannel.co/cat-habit-twerking-experts-reveal-why/?4f1e054b-09ef-44dd-bb70-6f5325e49f62=1

Hambly, M. (n.d.). *Why do cats purr?* New Scientist. https://www.newscientist.com/question/why-do-cats-purr/

Is my cat's kneading normal? (n.d.). Aaha. https://www.aaha.org/your-pet/pet-owner-education/ask-aaha/is-my-cats-kneading-normal/#:~:text=Kneading%20to%20convey%20comfort%20%E2%80%94%20Happy

Paoletta, R. (2017, November 27). *Why do cats follow you to the bathroom? We asked scientists.* Inverse. https://www.inverse.com/art icle/38778-why-do-cats-follow-you-to-bathroom

Shojai, A. (2022, April 15). *Do we know the reasons why cats purr?* The Spruce Pets. https://www.thesprucepets.com/cat-talk-cat-purri ng-553944

Shojai, A. (2023, June 29). *Why does your cat bring you dead animals?* The Spruce Pets. https://www.thesprucepets.com/cat-huntin g-gifts-553946

Sonoma,   S.   (2019,   March   10).   *Why   do   cats wiggle   their   butts   before   they   pounce?* Live   Science. https://www.livescience.com/64950-why-cats-wiggle-butts-b efore-pouncing.html#:~:text=%22It%20may%20also%20have%20a

Tamsin. (2021, December 22). *6 reasons why your cat won't let you sleep at night.* CatVills. https://catvills.com/cat-wont-let-me-sleep/

WebMD Editorial Contributors. (2023, March 16). *Nighttime activity in cats.* WebMD. https://www.webmd.com/pets/cats/nightti me-activity-cats

Why do cats bring you dead animals as gifts? (n.d.). Purina. https://www.purina.co.uk/articles/cats/behaviour/common-questio ns/why-do-cats-bring-you-dead-animals#:~:text=Your%20cat%20bri nging%20you%20mice

Made in the USA
Las Vegas, NV
13 December 2024

14162270R00046